EYE-POPPING
PHOTO
PUZZLES

Adam Ritchey

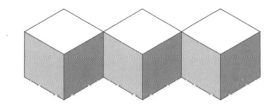

PUZZLE
WRIGHT
PRESS

An imprint of Sterling
Publishing Co., Inc.

www.puzzlewright.com

For Jackson

Puzzlewright Press and the distinctive Puzzlewright Press logo
are registered trademarks of Sterling Publishing Co., Inc.

Lot#:
2   4   6   8   10   9   7   5   3   1
04/10

Published by Sterling Publishing Co., Inc.
387 Park Avenue South, New York, NY 10016
© 2010 by Adam Ritchey
Distributed in Canada by Sterling Publishing
C/o Canadian Manda Group, 165 Dufferin Street
Toronto, Ontario, Canada M6K 3H6
Distributed in the United Kingdom by GMC Distribution Services
Castle Place, 166 High Street, Lewes, East Sussex, England BN7 1XU
Distributed in Australia by Capricorn Link (Australia) Pty. Ltd.
P.O. Box 704, Windsor, NSW 2756, Australia

Printed in China
All rights reserved

Sterling ISBN 978-1-4027-7079-1

For information about custom editions, special sales, premium and
corporate purchases, please contact Sterling Special Sales
Department at 800-805-5489 or specialsales@sterlingpublishing.com.

Contents

Introduction

Welcome to *Eye-Popping Picture Puzzles*! You'll need an exceptional eye, a marvelous mind, and an inkling of insight to solve these positively perplexing puzzles. Get ready to be stumped by skyscrapers, addled by airplanes, and befuddled by beaches. You might even find yourself bewildered by bugs, flummoxed by flowers, and unglued by umbrellas.

Eye-Popping Picture Puzzles features five different types of picture puzzles in four difficulty levels: Easy, Medium, Hard, and Killer. Here's how the puzzles work:

Spot the Differences 1

In this classic puzzle, you are challenged to find the differences between two seemingly identical photographs. Some of the changes are obvious while others are subtle. For each puzzle we've noted how many changes you can find.

Spot the Differences 2

Like the other type of Spot the Differences puzzle, here you'll again be looking for changes made in photographs. Except in this version, you are challenged to find only one difference each between the top photo and the four photos below. Each photo has a single, different modification than the others do.

Identical Images

These puzzles have one simple rule: Just find the two images that are completely identical. Or to think of it another way, it's "Spot the Lack of Differences"!

Missing Pieces

In this puzzle, we've taken one big photograph and pulled out twelve small squares from it. All you need to do is figure out where they belong! Use the grid coordinates as your guide. But, be warned: in the Hard and Killer levels, we've taken the additional step of rotating the squares. Some are rotated left, some are rotated right, and some are turned upside down.

Mixed-Up Images

And for the final puzzle type included in the book, we've taken three different but related photographs, chopped them into quarters, and then mixed them up. Your challenge is to discern the details that will allow you to put the images back together again.

That's all you need to know! To get started, just turn the page. Don't worry about being discombobulated or flustered. Just by holding this book you must be clever, adroit, astute, crafty, resourceful, savvy, and wise.

—Adam Ritchey

On the Road Again

Track Distraction

Strut Your Stuff

Gone With the Wind

EASY

14
differences

Answers
on page 131

Keep score:

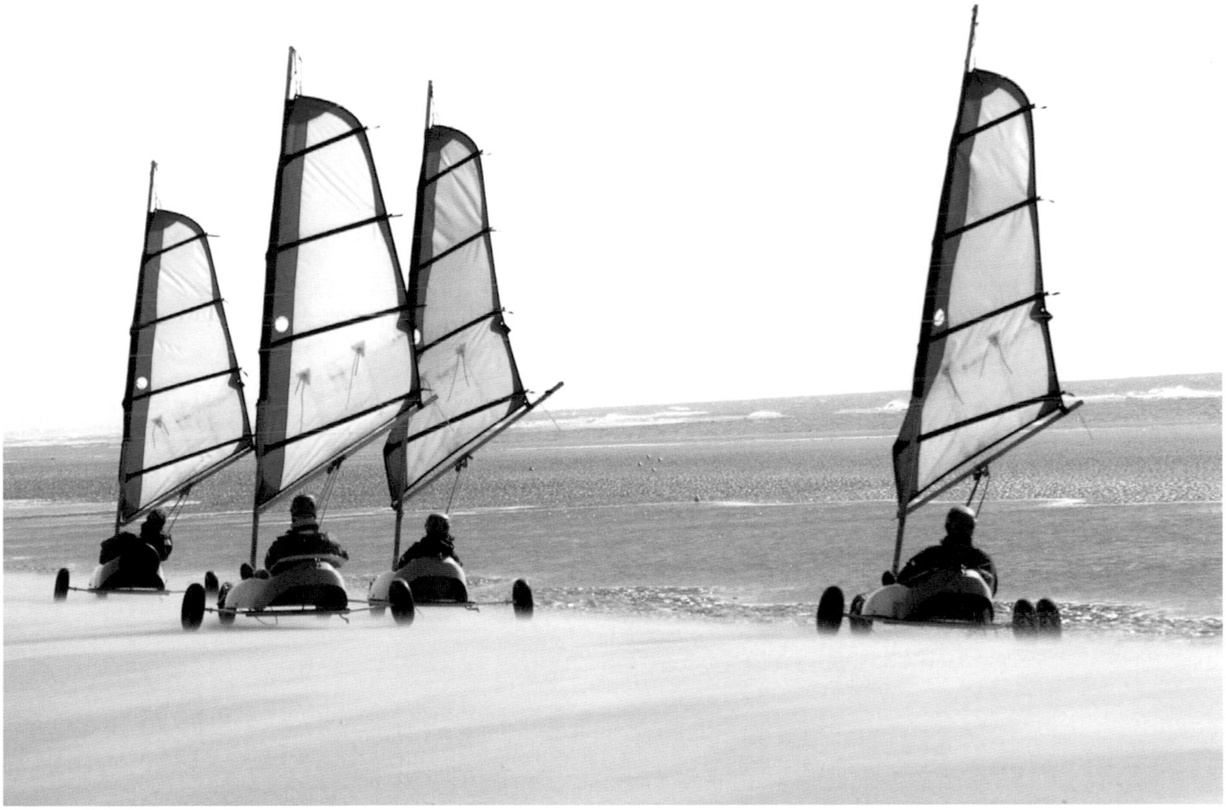

Dew Drops Do

Which two of these photos are exactly alike?

Answer on page 131

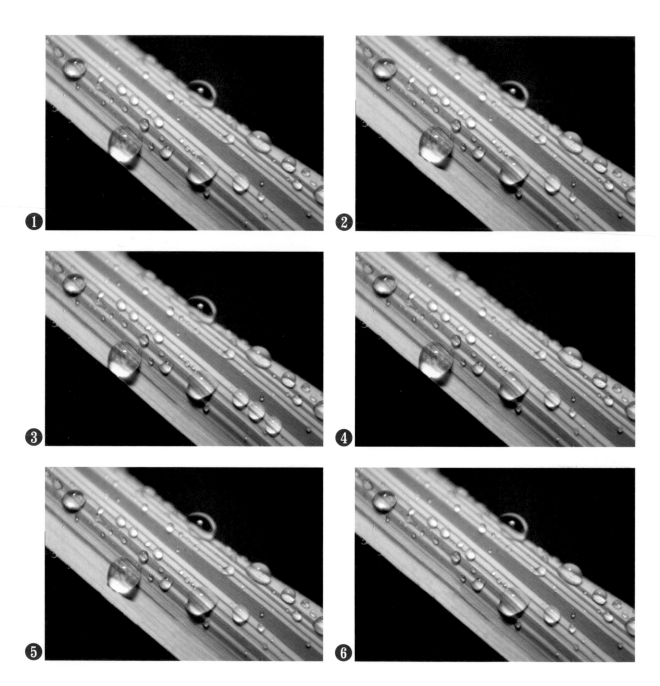

That's Cold-Blooded

Which two of these photos are exactly alike?

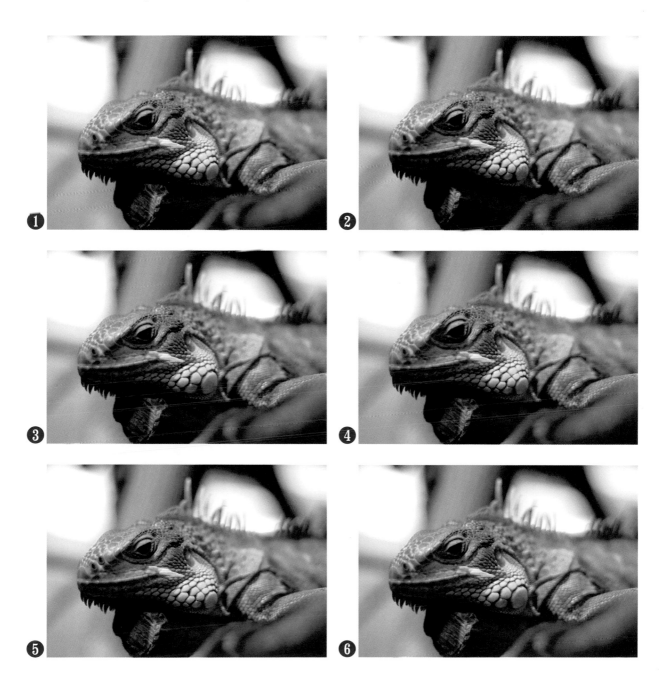

Answer on page 131

Up Where We Belong

Sweet ...

12
differences

Answers
on page 132

Keep score:

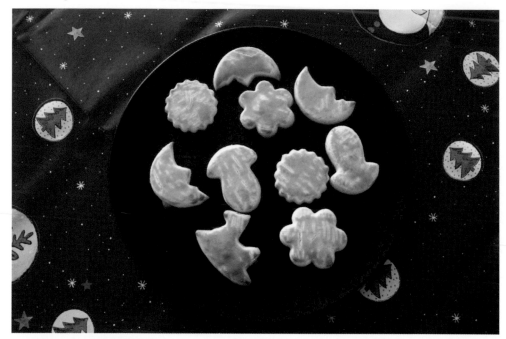

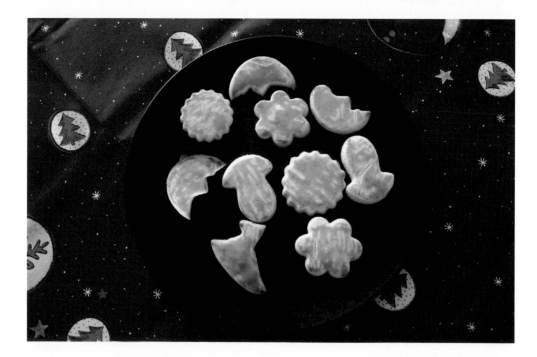

... and Sour

10
differences

Answers
on page 132

Keep score:

Colonial Conundrum

Airport Anarchy

Confounding Coinage

Can you locate the small images below in the large picture?

Answers on page 132

1: _____   7: _____

2: _____   8: _____

3: _____   9: _____

4: _____   10: _____

5: _____   11: _____

6: _____   12: _____

Grapes of Wrath

Can you locate the small images below in the large picture?

Answers on page 132

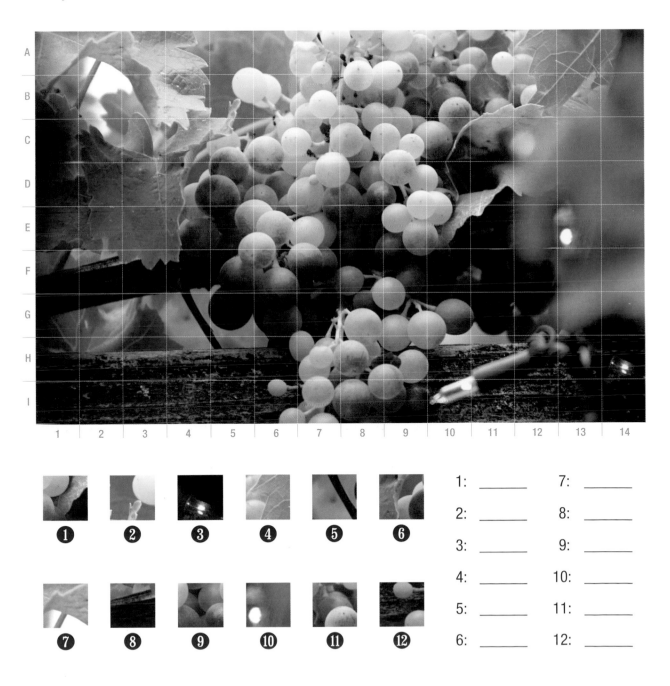

1: _____	7: _____
2: _____	8: _____
3: _____	9: _____
4: _____	10: _____
5: _____	11: _____
6: _____	12: _____

Here Comes the Sunflower

Out of Control

Troublesome Team

Meerkat Mystery

Each image has exactly one difference with the top photo. Can you find them all? Answers on page 133

Ladybug Bugaboo

Each image has exactly one difference with the top photo. Can you find them all? Answers on page 133

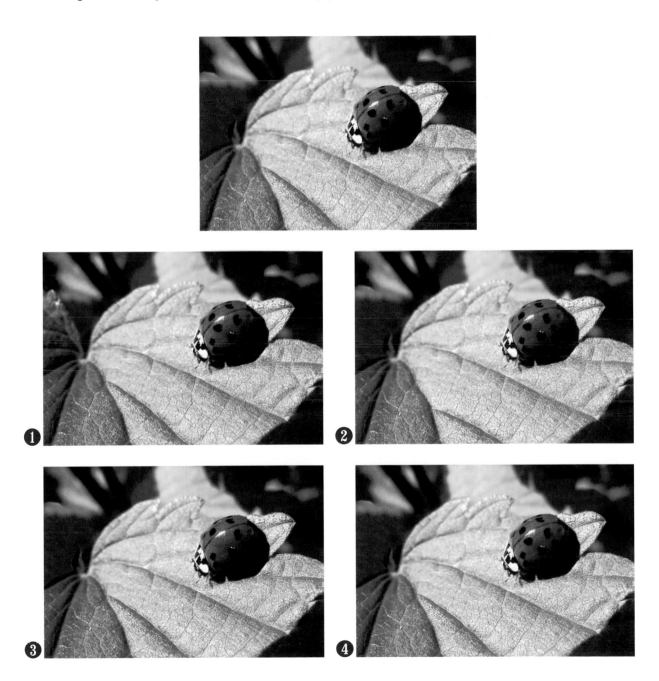

A Bridge Too Far

Answers
on page 133

Keep score:

Tropical Paradox

11
differences

Answers
on page 134

Keep score:

Time Trial

13
differences

Answers
on page 134

Keep score:

☐ ☐ ☐ ☐ ☐
☐ ☐ ☐ ☐ ☐
☐ ☐ ☐

Flower ...

Can you unscramble these three photos?

Answers on page 134

... Power

Can you unscramble these three photos?

Answers on page 134

Garage Mirage

Street Seen

Traffic Teaser

Maddening Moat

16
differences

Answers
on page 135

Keep score:

Tractor Trouble

Wind Power

Prepare for Landing

Little Friends

13
differences

Answers
on page 136

Keep score:

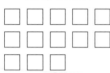

Big Friends

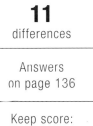

11
differences

Answers
on page 136

Keep score:

Stars ...

Which two of these photos are exactly alike?

Answer on page 136

... and Stripes

Which two of these photos are exactly alike?

Answer on page 136

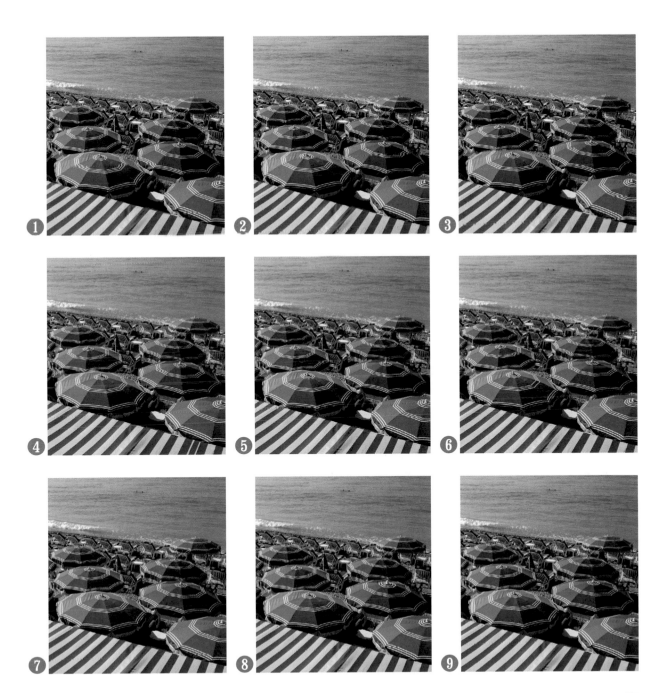

Row of Columns

Can you locate the small images below in the large picture?

Answers on page 136

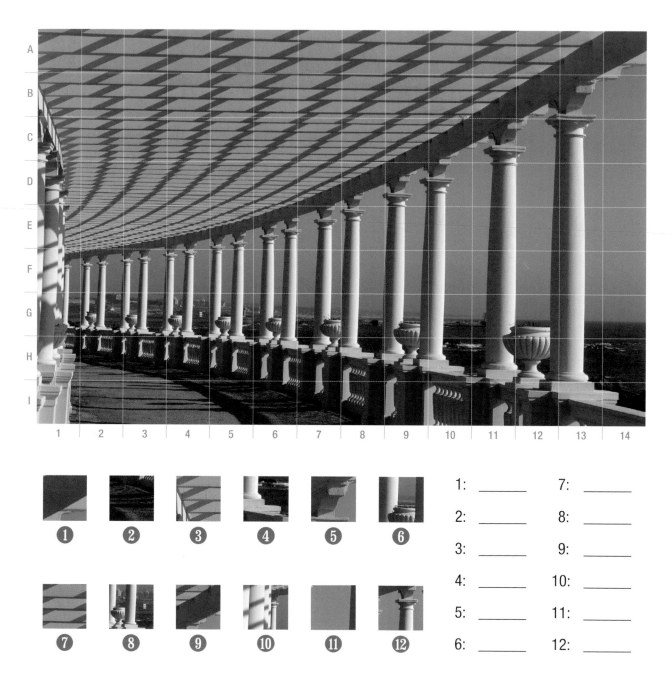

1: _____   7: _____

2: _____   8: _____

3: _____   9: _____

4: _____   10: _____

5: _____   11: _____

6: _____   12: _____

It Takes a Village

Can you locate the small images below in the large picture?

Answers on page 136

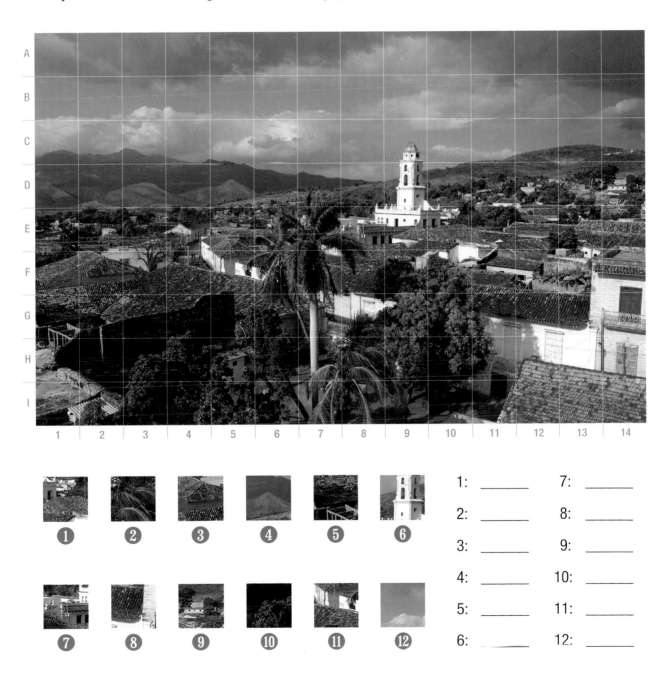

1: _____		7: _____
2: _____		8: _____
3: _____		9: _____
4: _____		10: _____
5: _____		11: _____
6: _____		12: _____

View With a Room

Architectural Anomalies

Home on the Range

16
differences

Answers
on page 137

Keep score:

Mangrove Mindboggler

13
differences

Answers
on page 137

Keep score:

A-Mazing Garden

11
differences

Answers
on page 137

Keep score:

Trumpet Stumper

Puppies ...

Each image has exactly one difference with the top photo. Can you find them all? Answers on page 138

... and Kittens

Each image has exactly one difference with the top photo. Can you find them all? Answers on page 138

Bike Flock

Can you unscramble these three photos?

Answers on page 138

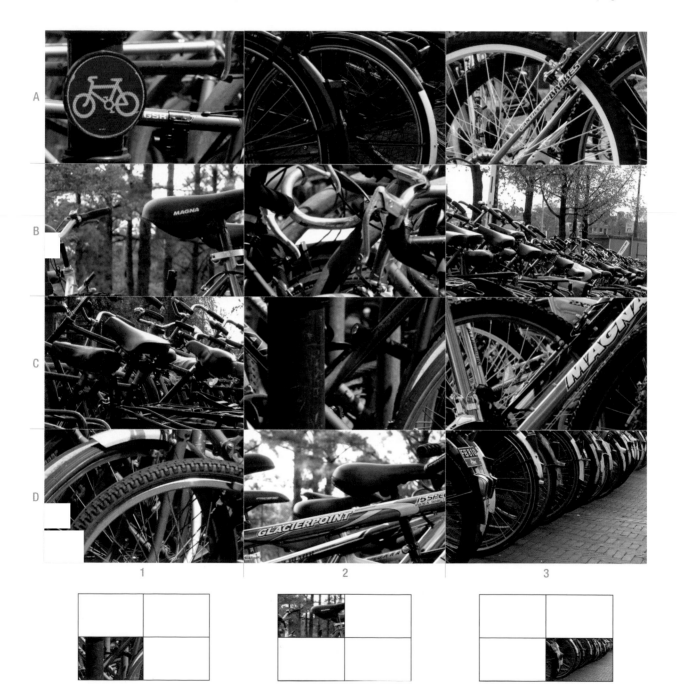

72

Head in the Clouds

Can you unscramble these three photos?

Answers on page 138

Night Vision

12
differences

Answers
on page 139

Keep score:

Pipe Predicament

Answers
on page 139

Keep score:

A Tough Nut to Crack

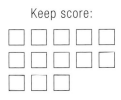

Enigmatic Electronics

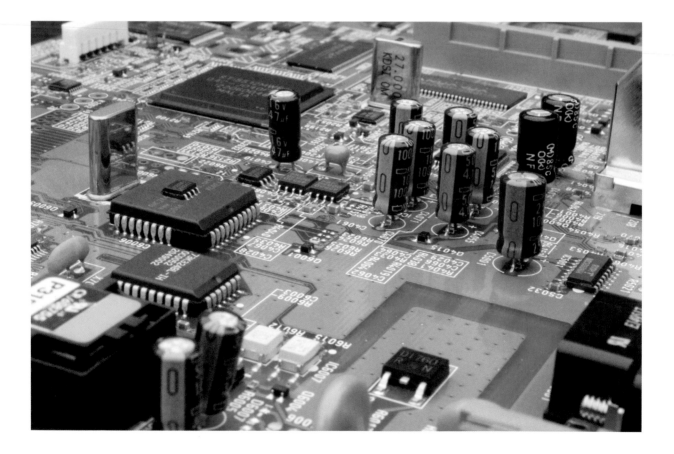

Picture Imperfect

Factory Showroom

Take a Seat

Which two of these photos are exactly alike?

Answer on page 140

Take a Stand

Which two of these photos are exactly alike?

Answer on page 140

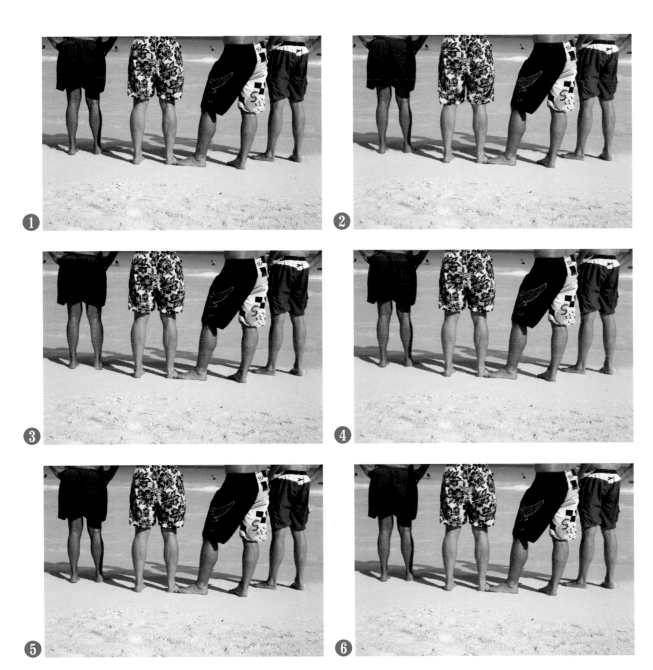

① ② ③ ④ ⑤ ⑥

Stamp of Approval

For a Rainy Day

Bamboozling

Can you unscramble these three photos?

Answers on page 140

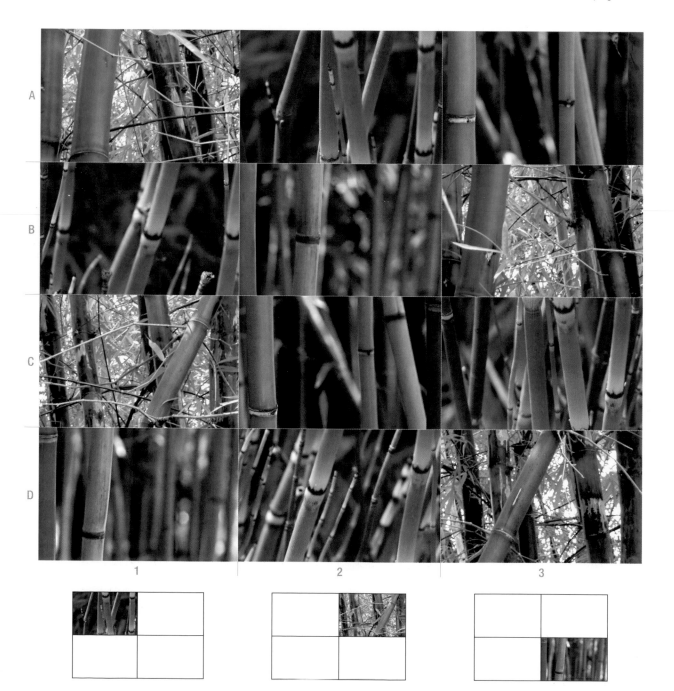

Marble Madness

Can you unscramble these three photos?

Answers on page 141

Winter Wonderland

14
differences

Answers
on page 141

Keep score:

Things Are Looking Up

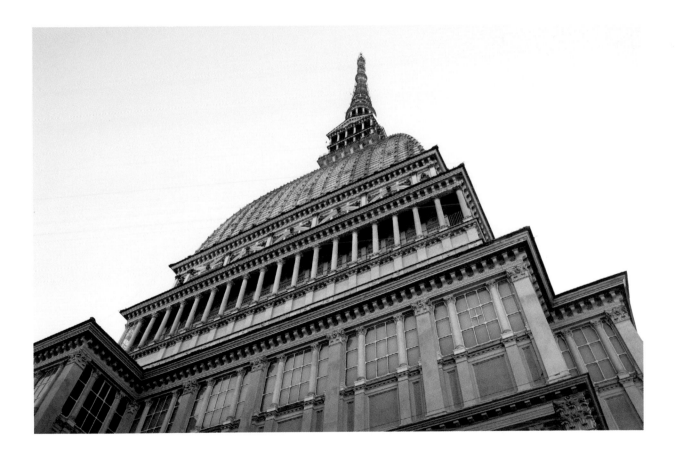

Saddle Sore

By Land ...

Each image has exactly one difference with the top photo. Can you find them all? Answers on page 141

... or by Sea

Each image has exactly one difference with the top photo. Can you find them all?   Answers on page 142

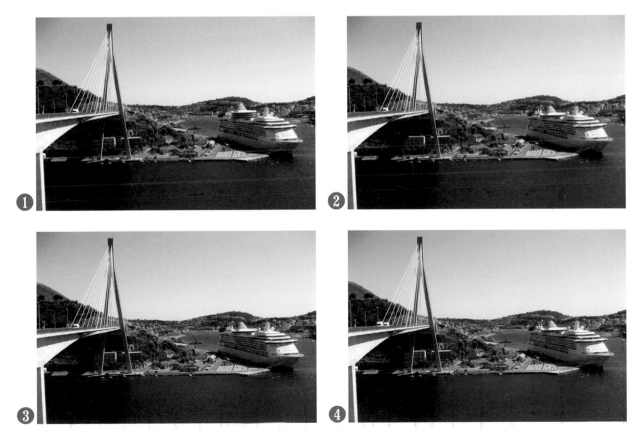

❶

❷

❸

❹

Light in the Piazza

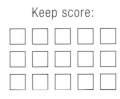

Migration Station

Kind of Blue

Can you locate the small images below in the large picture? Some may be rotated.   Answers on page 142

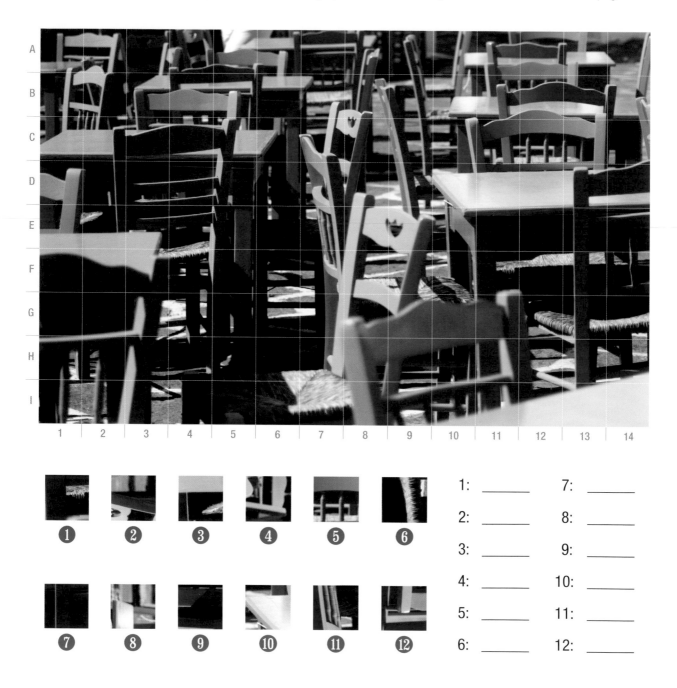

1: _____   7: _____

2: _____   8: _____

3: _____   9: _____

4: _____   10: _____

5: _____   11: _____

6: _____   12: _____

Luck of the Straw

Can you locate the small images below in the large picture? Some may be rotated.

Answers on page 142

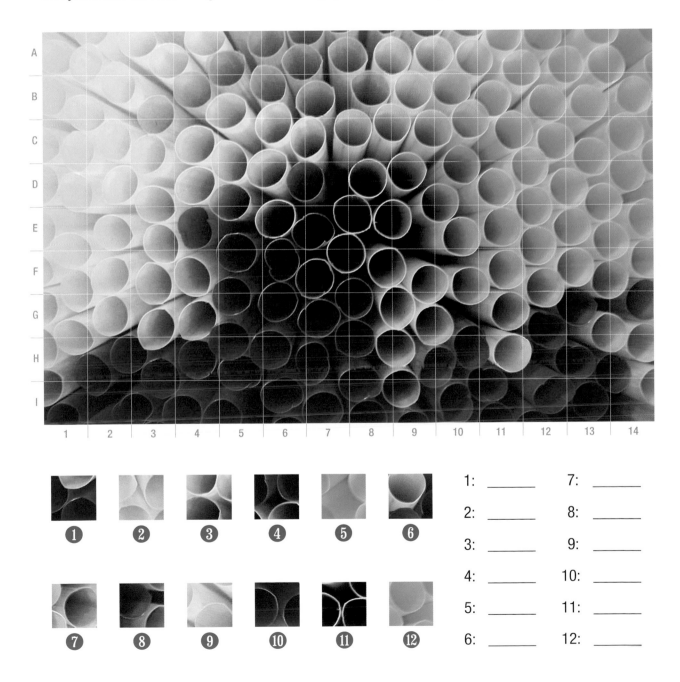

1: _____   7: _____

2: _____   8: _____

3: _____   9: _____

4: _____   10: _____

5: _____   11: _____

6: _____   12: _____

A Time to Reflect

City Lights

Poolside Poser

Once More Unto the Beach

Flummoxed by Flowers

Can you locate the small images below in the large picture? Some may be rotated.

Answers on page 143

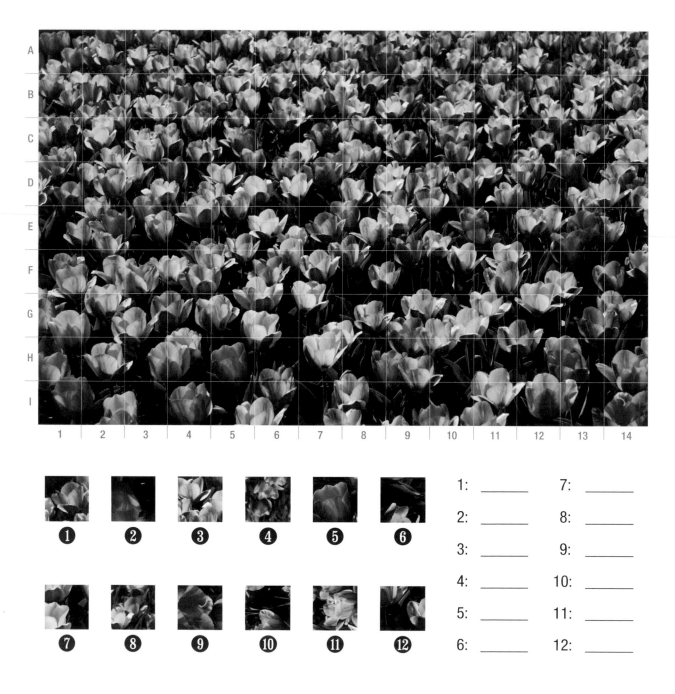

1: _____   7: _____

2: _____   8: _____

3: _____   9: _____

4: _____   10: _____

5: _____   11: _____

6: _____   12: _____

Vexed by Vines

Can you locate the small images below in the large picture? Some may be rotated.   Answers on page 143

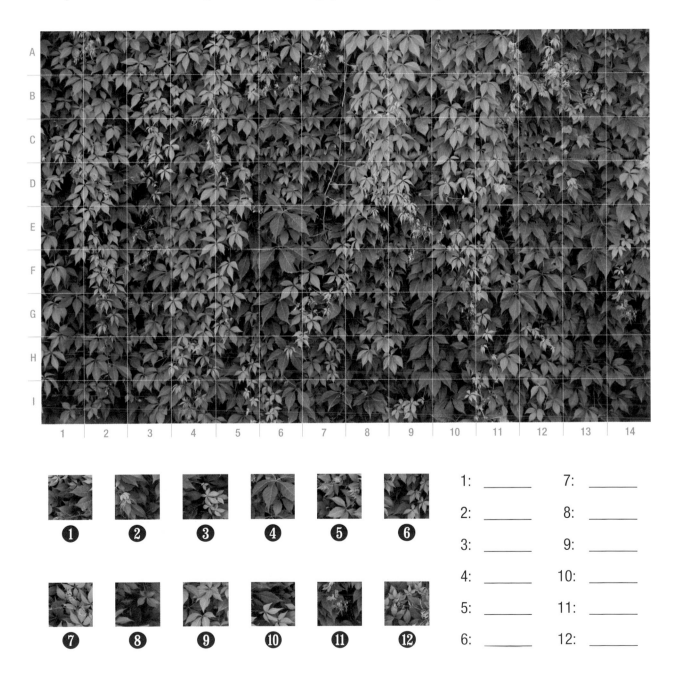

1: _____		7: _____
2: _____		8: _____
3: _____		9: _____
4: _____		10: _____
5: _____		11: _____
6: _____		12: _____

A Lot of Parking

119

Hall Monitor

Each image has exactly one difference with the top photo. Can you find them all? Answers on page 143

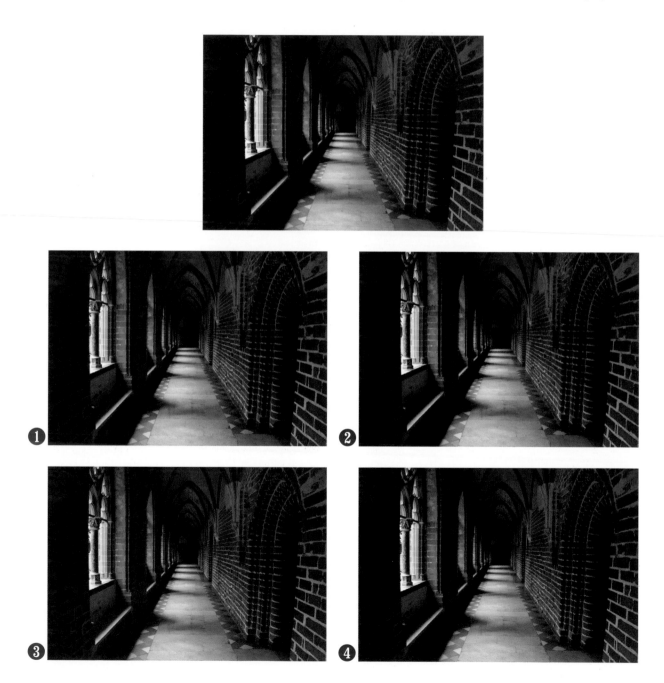

Blooming Difficult

Each image has exactly one difference with the top photo. Can you find them all? Answers on page 143

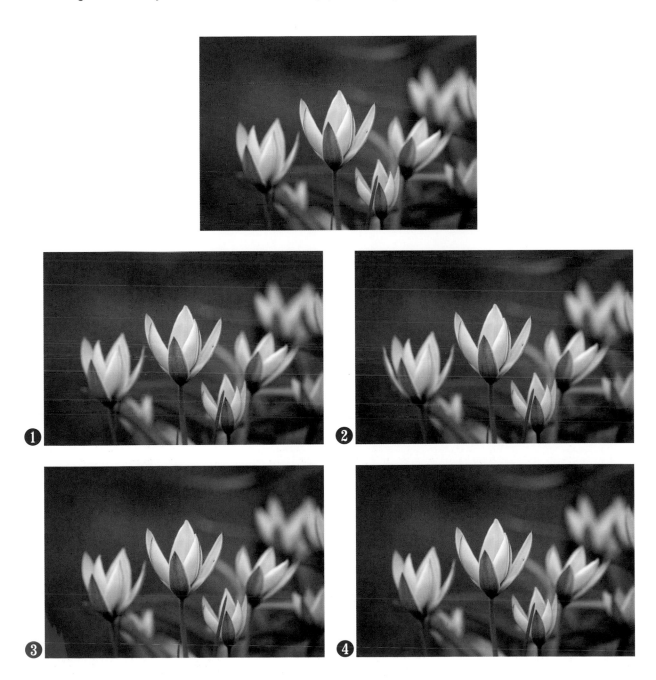

Gridlock Shock

Keep score:

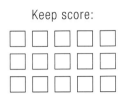

Bead-Dazzled

Eerie Canal

Dig In!

ANSWERS

On the Road Again

Track Distraction

Strut Your Stuff

Gone With the Wind

Dew Drops Do

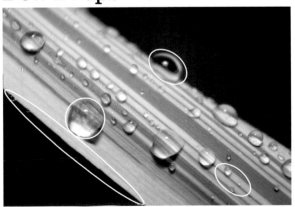

Images 2 and 5 are alike.

That's Cold-Blooded

Images 3 and 6 are alike.

Up Where We Belong

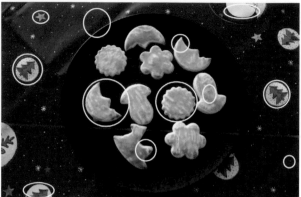

Sweet ...

... and Sour

Colonial Conundrum

Airport Anarchy

Confounding Coinage

1:	D5	5:	B14	9:	B10
2:	B3	6:	F5	10:	H8
3:	G13	7:	H3	11:	F2
4:	E10	8:	D9	12:	D14

Grapes of Wrath

1:	E10	5:	G4	9:	D8
2:	B5	6:	D4	10:	E13
3:	H14	7:	A2	11:	B10
4:	A12	8:	F2	12:	I6

Here Comes the Sunflower

Out of Control

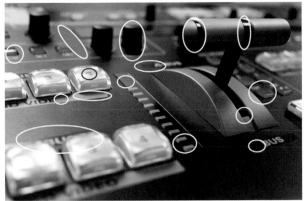

Troublesome Team

Meerkat Mystery

Ladybug Bugaboo

A Bridge Too Far

Tropical Paradox

Time Trial

Flower ...

C1	D1
B1	A1

D2	B2
C2	A2

B3	D3
A3	C3

... Power

D1	C3
A1	B2

A2	B3
C1	D2

D3	B1
A3	C2

Garage Mirage

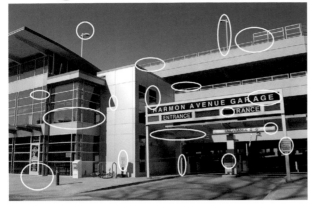

Street Seen

Traffic Teaser

Maddening Moat

Tractor Trouble

Wind Power

135

Prepare for Landing

Little Friends

Big Friends

Stars ...

Images 4 and 6 are alike.

... and Stripes

Images 3 and 5 are alike.

Row of Columns

1:	A14	5:	B13	9:	C10
2:	I6	6:	G9	10:	F1
3:	B1	7:	B4	11:	D12
4:	H10	8:	G4	12:	E7

It Takes a Village

1:	E10	5:	G1	9:	D14
2:	H8	6:	D9	10:	H3
3:	F2	7:	E8	11:	F5
4:	D5	8:	G13	12:	B3

View With a Room

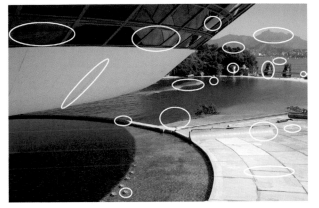

Architectural Anomalies

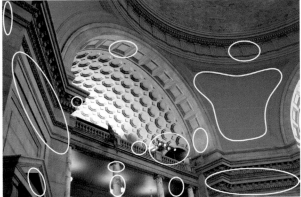

Home on the Range

Mangrove Mindboggler

A-Mazing Garden

Trumpet Stumper

Puppies ...

... and Kittens

Bike Flock

A1	B2
C2	D1

B1	D2
A3	C3

C1	B3
A2	D3

Head in the Clouds

A3	B1
C2	D1

D3	C1
B3	A2

B2	A1
C3	D2

Night Vision

Pipe Predicament

A Tough Nut to Crack

Enigmatic Electronics

Picture Imperfect

Factory Showroom

Take a Seat

Images 2 and 5 are alike.

Take a Stand

Images 1 and 6 are alike.

Stamp of Approval

For a Rainy Day

Bamboozling

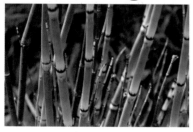

A2	B1
C3	D2

A1	C1
B3	D3

A3	B2
C2	D1

Marble Madness

A1	B3
D2	C1

D1	C3
B2	A3

A2	B1
C2	D3

Winter Wonderland

Things Are Looking Up

Saddle Sore

By Land ...

... or by Sea

Light in the Piazza

Migration Station

Kind of Blue

1:	F11	5:	C12	9:	F5
2:	C8	6:	G14	10:	D10
3:	E2	7:	E13	11:	E7
4:	A2	8:	B10	12:	B5

Luck of the Straw

1:	H3	5:	A14	9:	B3
2:	G1	6:	H11	10:	F5
3:	D5	7:	B8	11:	E8
4:	H8	8:	G13	12:	D14

A Time to Reflect

City Lights

Poolside Poser

Once More Unto the Beach

Flummoxed by Flowers

1:	E7	5:	H5	9:	I14
2:	I1	6:	E1	10:	E14
3:	D5	7:	G6	11:	C3
4:	A13	8:	B9	12:	F8

A Lot of Parking

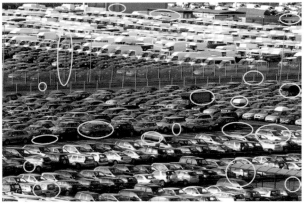

Vexed by Vines

1:	F8	5:	A6	9:	B10
2:	D13	6:	H5	10:	F5
3:	I9	7:	D2	11:	G14
4:	E6	8:	I1	12:	B13

Hall Monitor

Blooming Difficult

Gridlock Shock

Bead-Dazzled

Eerie Canal

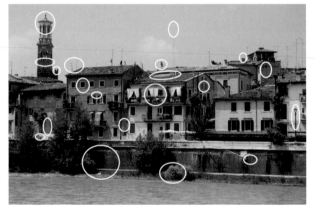

Dig In!